UNDERST

15–17
year olds

THE TEENAGE YEARS

UNDERSTANDING

15–17 year olds

Jonathan Bradley
and
Hélène Dubinsky

of

THE TAVISTOCK CLINIC
Series Editor: Elsie Osborne

ROSENDALE PRESS

First published in Great Britain in 1994 by:
Rosendale Press Ltd
Premier House, 10 Greycoat Place
London SW1P 1SB

Design by Pep Reiff
Production Edward Allhusen
Typeset by Ace Filmsetting Ltd
Printed in the United Kingdom by The Cromwell Press

British Library Cataloguing in Publication Data
A catalogue record for this book is available from
The British Library

ISBN 1 872803 75 X

The Tavistock Clinic, London, was founded in 1920, in order to meet the needs of people whose lives had been disrupted by the First World War. Today, it is still committed to understanding people's needs though, of course, times and people have changed. Now, as well as working with adults and adolescents, the Tavistock Clinic has a large department for children and families. This offers help to parents who are finding the challenging task of bringing up their children daunting and has, therefore, a wide experience of children of all ages. It is firmly committed to early intervention in the inevitable problems that arise as children grow up, and to the view that if difficulties are caught early enough, parents are the best people to help their children with them.

Professional Staff of the Clinic were, therefore, pleased to be able to contribute to this series of books to describe the ordinary development of children, to help in spotting the growing pains and to provide ways that parents might think about their children's growth.

THE AUTHORS

Jonathan Bradley is a Consultant Child Psychotherapist and Senior Tutor within the Adolescent Department of the Tavistock Clinic. He is also Head of Psychotherapy Services within Community Child Health, in Hackney, East London. He has an academic background in Psychology and also taught adolescents before training in Child and Adolescent Psychotherapy. His current interests range from individual psychotherapy to consultation with professional staff and institutions. Jonathan Bradley is married with three children.

Hélène Dubinsky is a Consultant Child Psychotherapist and Senior Tutor within the Adolescent Department of the Tavistock Clinic. As well as providing long-term psychotherapy to individual adolescents, she takes a special interest in the Young Peoples Counselling Services which offers focused short-term counselling to adolescents in need Hélène Dubinsky is married with an adolescent daughter.

We would like to thank Mrs Polly Hering for her time and assistance with this book.

CONTENTS

INTRODUCTION

Your fifteen-to-seventeen year olds will take you on a challenging but emotionally difficult ride. This is a time of physical and emotional upheaval and growth for them. Teenagers of this age are searching for a new identity, but on the way encounter a lot of confusion and contradictions within themselves. A 'child' and a more 'grown-up' self co-exist and alternate in unexpected and unpredictable ways. Indeed, parents may feel that teenagers are, like little children, impulsive, omnipotent and demanding of instant gratification. But they also have a capacity for strong, passionate emotions, a devotion and concern for good causes, and a growing intellectual capacity to question received ideas as well as to develop their own. They are hungry for space and freedom and, as they grow, will gradually learn that growing up also means taking responsibility for their actions. Teenagers are beset with uncertainties and questions about themselves: "Who are they?" "What will they become?" "What is their place in the world?". We share similar uncertainties about them, but also about ourselves as parents. They constantly challenge our way of thinking and our authority so that we wonder how to protect them without stifling them, how to understand and support them by being alive to their feelings and experiences.

This book is not intended to be used as a manual, as if your teenager could be compared against a check list of strengths and weaknesses, or worse still, in which you will be given detailed lists of do's and don't's. You will be very much more aware than we can be of the many different aspects of your teenager's personality. There are no general recipes. Sometimes however, it is possible to be so close that it is difficult to see what is going on. Hopefully, the themes we address in this book will help to provide an overall picture, though some parts may be more directly relevant than others to your particular situation. Given that teenagers develop in markedly different ways, we hope that examples drawn from incidents involving fifteen-to-seventeen year olds will let you see the kind of problems that other teenagers and parents have been confronted with and how they resolved them.

CHAPTER ONE

THE SEARCH FOR A NEW
IDENTITY

Fifteen-to-seventeen year olds are gradually moving away from childhood towards a period of ever greater vulnerability, change and confusion. From the beginning, their sense of self develops through their experiences with those closest to them. As children, they needed security, love and attention, boundaries, and a space for free activity within which their fantasies, wishes and needs could be explored. The needs of teenagers are not fundamentally different. However, they need much more space beyond the world of the family if their identity is to be developed. Teenagers let it be known that the need to have their own space and to be recognized as young adults is paramount. They are looking for new ways of being, behaving and looking. This search for a new identity is full of detours, with dramatic shifts from childlike feelings to those of an adult. They are torn, full of uncertainties about their identity and of what they want to be. They often suffer from not feeling sincere because their plans and feelings change so much. A long time is needed before the fifteen-to-seventeen year old can feel that particular behaviour and values belong to them, really expressing who they are.

School and society at large are often perceived as threatening to undermine this vital endeavour to assert the need for their own space and to be recognised as young adults. Teenagers may feel that they have to break away from their family. Fierce battles develop, as they complain that all that has been received to date is inadequate and needs to be rejected. This is a time of conflicts, grievances and the settling of scores. They often complain bitterly that parents, teachers and all other authority figures are stopping them from growing up, from asserting their individuality or newly acquired power and still trying to dominate their lives. As when they were children, teenagers feel a deep suspicion that adults not only have the monopoly of power and sexuality, but conspire to keep teenagers out of it. Suddenly, in arguments, deeply buried grievances, old jealousies and feelings of unfairness are stirred up: accusations for example, that another brother or sister was always the favourite, or that parents have in one way or another repeatedly failed them. We often reel under the pain of these dramatic accusations. We may feel hurt and resentful. But if we can evoke the memory of our own adolescent struggles, teenagers may be helped to tolerate these feelings better, and to talk about them when the storm has passed.

This is the time when endless, provocative discussions are

initiated by adolescents. Some incessantly provoke parents into endless political and sociological discussions, often with passion and idealism, sometimes with self-righteousness and arrogance, as they challenge parents' opinions and what they see as a stale, hypocritical way of life. These criticisms may be sharp and to the point, and difficult for parents to take. They show us that they want us to be stronger, more coherent and courageous, but also that they seek to define themselves as completely different from older generations. These arguments, however aggressive and provocative, may also be ways of trying to engage parents and keep a live bond going.

Natasha's parents, for example, are caring, hard-working people. Natasha, who was always a 'well-behaved, pleasing, good little girl', changed on turning fifteen. She dyed her hair bright red, would only dress in old torn jeans, and started to go out with a rebellious crowd of young people. She fought her parents every inch of the way for the right to be different from them. Although she avoided having meals with her parents and refused to go on family outings, she would tear down the staircase from her room every so often in an attempt to engage them in polemic discussions. She would inevitably take a radical, militant position, directly opposed to her father. These arguments would go on for hours. Natasha's father would end up feeling very provoked by his daughter's relentless questioning of all his attitudes and values. Although intense and bitter at times, the discussions seemed to be essential for Natasha, not only because she was able to assert her own identity as different from her parents, but because they reassured her of her parents' basic support and concern. They sensed that the fact that they took time to listen to her and put forward their own views was experienced as proof of this ongoing affection and care. Of course, they never were given the satisfaction of hearing this from Natasha.

Perhaps even more difficult for parents to tolerate than the incessant arguments just mentioned, are the times when teenagers withdraw into hostile and sulky depression. They may lock themselves in a messy room for hours, refuse to share meals with the family, or when there is no choice but to associate with them, remain silent and seemingly absent. At these times, it may be hard for parents to imagine that there still is a side of their teenager that both needs and wishes to remain in contact. The message seems to be: "Get off my back, give me a breather". However, if parents actually go along with this wish and give up the attempt to maintain communication, they risk being experienced as abandoning and rejecting. If both parents and teenagers find the strength to be able to weather these stormy times without a definite breakdown in their relationship, the outcome may be that from all this conflict, important growth and development will take place.

CHAPTER TWO

THE CHALLENGE TO FAMILY LIFE

The dramas of teenage life are played out with great intensity in the family. From the parents' perspective, this threatens to shatter the equilibrium of family life. From the teenagers' perspective, they are waging a justified struggle for greater freedom; if parents give in too much to their imperious demands, however, teenagers are liable to feel abandoned.

Mood swings

Adolescence is characterised by intense changes of mood. These can range from sulkiness to violent rages that may prove very disturbing for the whole family. Teenagers' attempts to deal with massive internal changes can render them so volatile that they magnify the smallest quarrel. Somehow, life seems to be lived at a more intense level than previously.

To adults, it may seem that the new day brings a new person with very little in common with the teenager who was there the day before. Parents may feel that they are receiving the kind of overflow of emotion they would have known how to respond to when their children were younger: with a hug, perhaps, or a teasing joke. Suddenly it feels more awkward: responding directly to troubles, particularly in an affectionate way such as with a hug or a kiss, can embarrass teenagers and lead them to feel that they are being treated like children. Of course, sometimes a reassuring physical gesture may be what they secretly long for.

To teenagers, however, parents can seem equally unreasonable. At times they may seem willing to discuss things, treating them like an adult; while at other times, they may seem unnecessarily strict, trying to turn the clock back to when their child was younger.

Issues which may seem trivial to parents take on huge importance for teenagers (as well as vice versa!). For example, while we may think of birthdays as an occasion for celebration, teenagers may feel that they point inexorably to adulthood and in particular, towards independent living and sexual maturity. At times, the thought of growing up and taking greater responsibility is welcome to teenagers, but at others, growing up is a frightening prospect, and they may wish to remain small and dependent.

Keeping boundaries

Sometimes, parents may feel that they have failed to establish any agreement about common rules in the household, because issues on which agreement seemed to have been reached are subjected to a repeated assault. Mary explained her dilemma as follows: she wanted to acknowledge her daughter Louise's wish for space, but she was also consumed with worry because at times, in wanting to stay out late, Louise seemed oblivious of danger. When questioned as to when she would come home, Louise would give a very vague answer, clearly irritated at being questioned. Phrases such as, "It's my life", and "I wish you would just trust me", did not calm Mary's anxiety, for although Louise fiercely defended her 'maturity', Mary could see she was at heart a vulnerable little girl. There seemed to be no way of communicating this without provoking arguments. Such confrontations happen all the time.

The pressure to relax boundaries can be enormous, as can be the temptation to impose inflexible arrangements suitable for a young child rather than a teenager. At times, it seems as though a situation could develop in which parents and teenagers are being presented with conflicting demands: on the one hand, the drive for separation and on the other hand, the drive for reassuring dependence. Both seem equally compelling. For example, if teenagers don't feel that they are being taken care of in a nurturing way, they may feel abandoned. While many adolescents will argue endlessly with whatever rules are imposed, it is very important that parents continue to set boundaries, and maintain a dialogue with their teenagers.

At times, this struggle can lead to division between parents. Jean and Charles described how they had been having trouble with

Thomas, their sixteen-year-old son. Recently, he had started leaving the family, spending long hours outside. Sunday lunch had until recently been a focal point for the family. Jean described how on one occasion she put a lot of effort into making a Sunday lunch which Thomas would appreciate. She made a point of asking him what he liked and went out of her way to prepare it. Just as the lunch was about to go on the table, Thomas appeared in his coat saying that he wouldn't be in for lunch (even though he had taken part in drawing up the menu) because he was seeing his girlfriend. Out he went. To her surprise, after Thomas had gone, Charles turned on her and said that she hadn't cooked the meal Thomas liked and that was why he had gone out. Although Jean appreciated that Charles too was feeling the strain of trying to hold on to Thomas and keep him within the family, it hurt her deeply because she had put such a lot of effort into preparing the meal. Although such incidents can seem trivial, they can cause enormous rifts within families. When they talked more about it, Charles saw that he had attacked Jean because he was hurt by Thomas' rejection, and she was an easy target.

Expectations and disillusionments

During these years, teenagers are making important life decisions. This may lead parents to look back on their own lives, including its disappointments or missed opportunities.

It is possible to overburden adolescents with hopes and expectations which don't originate from them. Parents may find it particularly infuriating to be faced with their adolescent's uncertainties, preoccupation with fashion, music or friends, rather than the 'motivated' adolescent they wish to see.

Michael, for example, had grown up under the shadow of his older sister. She had excelled in her studies, gaining admission to a prestigious university. Michael had performed much less well than she had, though he had still grown up with the expectation that he would follow in the family tradition of medicine. At least three generations in the family had been doctors or specialists in medicine. Michael was able to talk to a family friend, who was puzzled by the apparent contradiction between what seemed like an intellectual liveliness and the clear evidence that Michael was doing very badly at school. In general it appeared that for Michael, still a teenager, the future had already been mapped out. It seemed to him, that within the school he attended there were many teenagers who were quite clear about their own choice of career. By contrast, his choice of career was being predetermined by family tradition. A dutiful part of him was convinced that he must follow earlier generations. At the same time, it was quite apparent that he wouldn't be able to get sufficiently high grades to do this. More than this, he had managed to get himself into a position within the class structure whereby he was regarded as a non-performer, something of a class clown who could be relied upon to enliven the proceedings by not having finished homework and by producing colourful excuses. So the stated aim, that of following in his father's footsteps, was clung to, but it had a hollow ring to it.

Recently, Michael had started to talk about his own ambitions. On the whole, they were expressed negatively, more to do with what he didn't want to do rather than with positive interest. One suggestion he made was that he should leave school early rather than proceed to 'A' levels and university. When he talked it through, however, it became obvious that he was trying to put himself into a position where he couldn't possibly be asked to pursue the family profession. How could he do this if he was a failure? It seemed hard for him to think that qualifications could lead to another profession. Michael wasn't at all confident that if he did well in exams he would be able to resist the pressure to take up medical studies.

Interestingly, when the family friend, with Michael's permission, spoke to his parents about the pressure which he felt Michael was under, it became apparent that they were unaware of what a daunting task it was for him to be expected to follow in the family footsteps. Michael's mother had experienced similar pressures in her own life but she had been able to express her rebellion in a more forthright and obvious way. She was very disillusioned by what she felt was his lack of ambition and intellectual ability. The thought that there may have been a connection between poor performance and confusion about the future was frankly a new concept to her. Once accepted, however, she was able to use her insight to reopen discussions with him about the future. There was a remarkable leap in progress once it became clear that the future was his to shape, rather than a grim mould into which he would have to be pressed and fitted.

This example is not unique. Indeed, the theme of disillusionment coupled with despair which can develop between teenagers and parents when expectations fail to be fulfilled is a common experience, but it can be negotiated when dealt with sensitively.

The task for individual parents

At this time, teenagers are involved in much re-negotiation of their individual relationships to their fathers and mothers. Being able to define oneself in relation to the major figures in one's life, particularly parents, is an essential part of self-discovery and the building of personality. It is bewildering for parents and teenagers alike to discover that they are being pitched into bruising confrontations that seem worryingly reminiscent of battles in earlier years, but with less obvious solutions. Old ways of dealing with disagreements, particularly if they relied on greater strength or on the authority of seniority alone, now need to be re-thought because they can be experienced as unnecessarily provocative to the young adolescent.

Andrew, for example, a well developed seventeen-year-old boy, felt that when he was younger he at least knew where he stood as far as his father was concerned. He remembered vividly being confronted by his father about some petty stealing. He was eight at the time. He remembered having to look up at his father, who was a powerful though kindly man, and feeling afraid. Despite the fear, knowing where his father stood on issues of discipline must have been reassuring for Andrew. Recently, they had started having impromptu contests of strength. These would start off as something frivolous such as arm wrestling, but then would become much more serious than this. Andrew had become more and more frustrated at not being able to beat his father, however close he came to doing so. He was beginning to notice a change in his father's attitude. Whilst seemingly making light of it, his father had started to work much harder at his level of fitness, in particular, taking up weight training. And so Andrew too had begun to 'train', though it was only subsequently that he realised the significance of both he and his father getting themselves to peak condition in parallel, whilst they both studiously avoided arm wrestling contests. When the 'battle of the giants' finally came, Andrew triumphed. However, accompanying the sense of having won a famous victory was, curiously, a feeling of disappointment. Perhaps the security of believing in the 'strong' father of his childhood had been suddenly lost.

Clearly, Andrew and his father had become locked together in a relationship which was based on a struggle for dominance. In this scenario, if you aren't the dominant one, you are the 'loser'. Presumably, the struggle between them took on this stark form because they got stuck in their earlier pattern of relationship based on strength, and Andrew's father felt too threatened to give this up willingly. It was difficult for him to allow the development of his son without feeling 'dethroned'. The need to conquer his father physically was Andrew's response to an attitude that wasn't able to provide sufficient emotional space for a growing adolescent.

Such struggles between parents and their teenagers can take many forms. In the case of Maria it centred around school and home life. Though clearly able academically, she felt completely estranged from her parents. It was quite common for her not to talk to them for days on end and at times, to behave as if she didn't want to know them. Maria's parents invested a great deal towards her education. They wanted her to have a better education than themselves. Even though they were not well off, they had provided private tutoring from time to time. With a great deal of determination, they had managed to get her into a reputable state school, despite living outside the catchment area. Not only did they feel hurt by her apparent rejection of them, but also deeply disappointed that she rarely showed signs of enjoying school. Nonetheless various progress reports suggested she was performing well there. It was a different matter at home where she never invited her school friends. Maria was determined to 'hang out' with the children from her area, a lot of whom were 'fed up' with school. Her parents became very worried that she might be involved in drugs, and were concerned at their lack of contact with her once she came home. Maria, for her part, was adamant that she did not take drugs. With an air of confidence, she would declare that she didn't agree with them though many of her friends did take them in her presence. She felt she was able to stand her ground and that despite these differences she still had more in common with her friends at home than her friends at school.

It began to look as though Maria would drift into serious trouble in spite of her confidence that she knew what she was doing. It became clear that she was increasingly distancing herself from her academic side in favour of a much more confused aspect of herself. In her muddle she clung to a group of friends whose main bond was of feelings of resignation, despair and on the whole, lack of academic success. It was an environment that had much in common with the background of Maria's parents, and Maria recognised this.

It is hard to know precisely why there was such a degree of estrangement between herself and her parents. Perhaps one contributing factor was that she had felt plucked out of her natural social environment, albeit with the best of intentions, but without consultation as far as she was concerned. Her life seemed to present in dramatic form a struggle to fit in with the aspirations of her parents, particularly in the way she struggled at school and did well there, and at the same time, a need to find her own world which would allow her to attack her parents' ambitions for her.

Andrew and Maria both point to a very striking feature of family life where there are adolescents: on both sides of the divide, there can be great disillusionment and disappointment. These feelings would seem to be heightened when expectations have built up a great deal. With the best intention in the world, the wish to provide children with a much better opportunity in life than parents had themselves, can lead to a blurring of the boundary between an understandable wish to provide children with better opportunities, and a determination to relive life through them.

Mid-life crisis in parents

Many other pressures for parents can come about in a much more unacknowledged way. The very presence of a teenager so obviously at the threshold of adulthood, both sexually and in terms of career, can lead to parents feeling devalued. Being in the same household as somebody so obviously on the verge of new life can force parents to re-evaluate where they have got to. David, for example, was in his forties and had been quite happily married, as he saw it, for a number of years, though business pressures took him abroad a lot. But recently, since his eldest daughter of sixteen had become passionately involved with a boyfriend, he found himself looking critically at the circumstances under which he married. Increasingly, he felt he had been trapped and had missed the opportunity of youthful passion. He realised that he had kept himself within the family largely for the sake of his three children. It wasn't long before he started to have an affair with a much younger woman and, after a while, left his family for her. However, the affair didn't work out and in the end, after a painful time for all concerned, he returned to his family. On reflection, it seemed to him that his decision to leave was connected with seeing his teenage daughter's exuberant sensuality unfold and the consequent wish to reclaim his own adolescence and start afresh.

For other parents, having children reach adolescence can lead to a kind of mourning about the loss of the time when they were young parents with young children rather than the older parents of teenagers about to move away from home. This can be felt particularly deeply by women who have given up work to bring up their children and suffer a sense of emptiness as their teenagers gain independence.

Step-families

Christopher's father left the family when Christopher was five. Christopher has a sister, Harriet, two years older. Their father did at first maintain contact with them, seeing his children at weekends. Then gradually his visits became rare; he would make promises which he didn't keep and by the time Christopher's mother remarried, contact between father and the children was virtually non-existent. Even before Christopher's parents had separated, Christopher had not seen much of his father who was either travelling or preoccupied with his work. In fact, Christopher used to get under his father's skin; he had been a very cuddly child, very close to his mother but very aggressive with his father whilst at the same time desperately wanting his attention. Here is Christopher reflecting on that time:

"When I was eight, I wished I could pretend Dad was still there. Then we would go and do something together, like riding a bike or swimming. My dad never paid that much attention to me. I had to wait until my step-father came along to learn how to swim. My step-father was awfully nice to me in the beginning. He still is, I guess. He would take me with him when he had things to do and he would explain to me the things I would need to know when I grew up and had a family of my own. He said women didn't understand these things. He made me feel important. My sister never got along with him. She was always suspicious of him and said he was an idiot. She was right, only I couldn't see that. I guess I was too busy pretending my dad was there once more, but it was the better, improved dad, the dream dad who was confident and secure as a man. He would know about airplanes, engines, horses and sailboats and feel comfortable with me standing next to him, my little hand in his large one. Anyway, my mum had married him so he couldn't be a moron, because she is clever. And she has tons of love for me. But my sister was right. My step-father *is* a moron. At fifteen, when I first realised that, I was already too old to want to hold his hand, but I did want to respect him and I couldn't. Not any more. All those things he had taught me wouldn't be much use after all because I didn't think I wanted to live a life like his, bragging that he knew all about women because men are more intelligent. He's not more intelligent than my mother – or me, for that matter. He thought he was pretty hot stuff, that everybody looked up to him and tried to live by his rules. I couldn't do that. I had lost my respect for him. So I was sad and confused. I wished I could respect him once again. I wished things could be like they once were, but I knew they couldn't, not ever. Also, I was furious with my mother. How could she have done such a thing to us? We were doing well before she got married. I realise I was too small to be much use, but we did get along, and my sister and I did try to help. Now, I felt I was old enough to be the man in the house, but it was too late, we were stuck with my moron step-father.

I decided not to speak any more, not when we were having dinner all together, because he aggravated me. Everything he said, everything he did confirmed my worst suspicions. My sister was already bitching at him all the time. I didn't want to make matters worse or make my mother sad by showing her that I agreed with my sister. I was angry with at my mother. I couldn't understand what she was doing with this man her children hated. But I didn't want to make her sad or make things worse than they already were, because if I had spoken I would have exploded. I would have shouted insults at him and spat in his face (which probably wouldn't have been a very good idea). My mother wondered what was wrong with me. She asked my sister if I was in love with a classmate. In love indeed! More like 'in hatred'.

I didn't have to keep my policy of silence every night because my step-father belonged to a men's club where he used to spend some evenings. We had so much fun then. We would make sandwiches in the kitchen, pile them up on a tray and bring them to the couch in front of the telly. We would 'bundle up' on the couch and even let the dog climb aboard. My step-father would never have allowed this. We would watch TV, stuff our faces and chat. I loved those evenings. So did my mother – I could just see it in her smile and the fact that she never would have done this when my step-father was in the house. So why was he in the house in the first place? I never could understand this: I think I never will."

Christopher shows us, in his ironic monologue, his pining for a father. When his mother remarried, he transferred his longing onto his step-father with the hope that he would now fulfil all his expectations. Indeed for a while, his step-father did live up to this high ideal. At fifteen, be became totally disillusioned with this man whom he had trusted and looked up to. Like most adolescents, Christopher had become, with the aid of his sister, very critical in a quite arrogant way, scrutinizing all the flaws, some real, some imagined ones, of his step-father's character. At the time of adolescence, as we have seen throughout this book, earlier conflicts of authority, rivalry, of trust versus distrust, hope versus disillusion-ment, love versus bitter resentment, become exacerbated. These conflicts can be all the more intense when a step-father or step-mother is involved because of the underlying, perhaps unresolved, problems the younger child might have had in accepting step-parents in the first place. Christopher seemed to welcome the presence of his step-father wholeheartedly and his rivalry with him for his mother's attention went unnoticed, only to surface later with all the more virulence. It is very important to bear in mind the complexity of feelings that accepting a new partner and sometimes new step-brothers and sisters can arouse in a child. There is always a wish on parents' part to make the transition as smooth as possible and to become a 'happy family', but there is a danger that in doing this, more problematic aspects of this process might be glossed over. Had Christopher's mother and step-father been aware of his anger and pain, not only at having lost his real father but now, in his eyes, of losing his privileged relationship with his mother, they might have been able to help him to try to come to terms with his emotions. Christopher might not have had to deny them and might have prevented so violent an eruption in adolescence. If feelings can be expressed and thought about, the members of the new family might be more able to give each other support and to respect the need for individual space.

CHAPTER THREE

THE TEENAGER AND SCHOOL

Crucial years

The years from fifteen to seventeen cover some of the most crucial events in academic development. At fifteen, generally speaking, teenagers will still not have taken their first public exams (GCSE). By the time they are sixteen, some may have decided to leave school while others may choose to stay on and take 'A' levels with thoughts of pursuing further education. Many factors will have an influence: teenagers' own values, interests and motivation; their academic ability and the kind of work they want to do later; parents' expectations and financial situation; the values of the teenagers' group of friends; the influence of teachers and school; and above all, the teenager's state of mind at this particular time. Understandably, young people may need assistance to help them think about the decisions they will have to make concerning their education.

The challenge of exams

For those teenagers who stay on at school, exams will be an increasingly important part of the scene. Results determine whether they go into further education and what kind of job they are likely to get, so the pressure to succeed brings overwhelming anxieties. They may feel that it is not only their academic competence, but their whole inner life which is being judged. It may seem as if the examination will decide on whether they are 'good enough' to be allowed to take their place in society, or whether by contrast, they are deeply flawed as human beings, bound to be a disappointment to themselves, teachers and parents. If you are afraid that your value as a person is to be decided by the way you perform in exams, then there is a great temptation to rubbish exams, run away from them and turn to some excitement which gives instant gratifications. Alternatively, some adolescents will withdraw into a sleepy, dazed, depressed state. Also, as was suggested earlier in the example of Michael, parents may put too much pressure on their son or daughter, because they are trying to realise unfulfilled ambitions through them.

Susan, for example, had always been a very diligent and studious pupil who wanted to train as a primary school teacher. She was committed to her studies and found them enjoyable, despite occasional feelings of anxiety, related to doubts about her capacity to complete her work to the teacher's satisfaction. However as her mock 'A' levels drew near, she became very depressed, staying in bed until mid-afternoon, refusing to go to school and maintaining that her English teacher was 'out to get her' no matter how hard she worked. She felt there was no point in doing anything at all. For Susan, taking to her bed seemed to express a wish to return to being a little child.

The sudden change in her attitude may have had something to do with changes and upheavals in her family; her elder brother, to whom she was very close, had left home to go and live with his girlfriend in another town and her maternal grandfather had died after a long illness. Susan's mother, herself depressed over her father's death and her eldest son leaving home, would get irritated and angry over the endless arguments with her. Susan steadfastly refused to listen to her parents. It became clear that the approaching exams were overwhelming at a time when she already felt very vulnerable. When Susan's parents realised that they were not managing to help her overcome her apprehension and despair about school, they thought of asking Susan's favourite aunt to talk to her about it. For some time, this aunt became a very important part of Susan's life, and Susan seemed to confide in her whilst remaining distant from her mother. Her mother was able to tolerate this and realised that Susan was slowly picking herself up. Eventually Susan managed to go back to school though she continued to need support. From time to time, Susan would be overcome by discouragement and a recurrent wish to give it all up, since she had now fallen behind in her studies. Eventually, with a lot of support from parents, aunt and school, she managed to face the daunting challenge of her exams.

Firm support of Susan was an essential contribution to her

overcoming the crisis. Giving in to her depression and giving up her studies would have deepened Susan's feeling that she didn't have it in her to face difficulties.

The development of critical judgement

Between fifteen and seventeen, important changes are taking place in the way thinking and learning occur. Simon, for example, had done reasonably well in his GCSE examinations. He admitted freely that he had done so by paying attention to that part of his course work which counted towards his overall grade. He had worked very hard during the weeks before the exams and had benefitted from his good memory and coolness under exam conditions. It was difficult for him to say which subjects were his favourites, though on the whole, they tended to coincide with teachers he liked and those who provided him with easily digested facts. When he began to study 'A' levels however, he began to encounter very different demands. The teacher for English Literature had taught him earlier, and Simon had thought he would do as well as previously. But it quickly became apparent to him that for the first time in his life, he was encountering real difficulties. Unusually, he wasn't able to get out of the problem by relying on his memory which had got him out of trouble before. The particular area of difficulty was that of literary criticism. The teacher had discussed the general principles of criticism, but Simon found it very difficult to think for himself and to give his own views about literature. His first attempts had not been good. The teacher, a friendly person, had shown him how he had simply summarised the play they were reading rather than assessing the central characters. Simon tried again, and this time expressed very strong views about the play. However, to his frustration, his opinions were said to express views which weren't supported by the text itself.

Simon's difficulty seems to pinpoint a particular challenge to thinking which fifteen-to-seventeen year olds are facing. They may be expected, perhaps for the first time, to think critically and to substantiate their opinions in a coherent manner. Forming a logical and dispassionate personal opinion can feel very difficult: teenagers may not know what they generally think and if they have an idea, it may be hard for them to differentiate between critical thinking and a need simply to oppose 'received' knowledge.

Leaving school/staying on

Between the ages of fifteen and seventeen, some teenagers will finish school out of necessity or by choice. Indeed, a number of teenagers who as children were proud to achieve good results at school seem now to give up on their studies. They can't be bothered any more, they hate school, finding it boring, a total waste of time. They become critical, rebelling against the school system. They feel 'got at', infantilised by teachers and parents who press them to do school work, to make long-term plans for the future when teenagers may well feel that the world, and freedom, are beckoning. They may disengage from studies for a variety of reasons: because they are questioning, perhaps seeing more clearly the shortcomings of school, the lack of job opportunities in the future, or perhaps are fearful of competitive exams.

For many teenagers, it is particularly difficult to settle down to what may well seem many more years of additional study when instead they could leave school immediately, earn some money and be relatively free of cares, at least in the immediate future. Newspapers and magazines are full of stories about talented young people in the music or sports worlds who rebelled and left school as early as possible to follow their inclinations. They are shown surrounded by the trappings of fame and fortune. The feeling conveyed is that they broke free, away from the endless humiliation of meaningless, boring homework and from the repressive control of parents and teachers. It can be difficult for young people, in the face of such pressure, to become involved in studies for their own sake or even to regard further study as an investment for the future.

John, for example, described how frustrated he felt about belonging to a local football team in which many of the members had already left school. They were the ones with money, it seemed, whereas he (despite his weekly allowance) felt himself to be totally dependent on his father. His frustration was compounded by realizing that he wanted to continue studies which he liked, but he could see no end to seemingly endless dependency and personal poverty. Although he didn't want to appear greedy, his increasing frustration led to bouts of rebellion at home which were looked upon as puzzling ingratitude. There seems to be no easy answer to the kind of dilemma John faced. He put up with the frustration of not being as 'financially' independent as his friends by gradually finding a weekend job which at least gave him some sense of being able to earn money of his own. For some teenagers, however, it is simply too difficult to deal with such frustrations without giving up their studies completely.

For example, when Tom was fifteen, he became very rebellious, critical and scathing towards his parents and school. He had always had a difficult relationship with his father, a high-flier who put considerable pressure on his son's academic achievements. Tom challenged authority in a provocative, arrogant way. He was a bright pupil, English being his best and favourite subject. However, his main interest began to shift from learning to becoming the natural leader of a group of boys. He became obsessed with wearing the 'right clothes', the 'right shoes', and having the 'right cool attitude' which entailed 'doing drugs'. In general, therefore, his chief preoccupation was to attract the envy and admiration of the other members of the gang. Though displaying total contempt for school which stood for authority and his father, he was secretly very worried that his work was deteriorating and that therefore his teachers could be critical and scathing towards his work. While sitting his 'mock exams', John and a friend went out of the school to smoke during the break and decided there and then to give it all up. John never went back. He had a few jobs which he abandoned in anger and disgust. Then he joined a band which he really enjoyed, but got heavily involved in drugs. Although still very defiantly contemptuous towards education and some of his friends who had gone on with education, he was unhappy. He missed the discipline and the challenge of his studies, particularly writing and thinking about books. He began to wonder whether he had been trapped by his own rebelliousness, letting himself down. Eventually at twenty, after some help, he went back to evening classes in further education.

Intimidation and bullying at school

Being bullied can be a cause of considerable fear, resentment and humiliation to an adolescent. Because most adolescents are intensely preoccupied by the image they project, and the impression they make on the rest of the group, they are particularly vulnerable to being teased by other boys and girls, who will pick on vulnerable targets as a way of denying their own helplessness. There can be 'nick names', perhaps because of some physical characteristics such as being too fat, too thin, or because of some gossip, invented facts, sexual attributes, or to do with family or race. The bullied adolescent may develop a sense of injustice and deep resentment and this can lead to absenteeism or total refusal to go to school. Parents and teachers sometimes want to ignore the problem or hope adolescents will be able to stand up for themselves. But adolescents can only address the problem if they have the internal strength to do so, have the insight to see what they are contributing themselves, and if the external situation is not sufficiently serious to require specialist help.

In the first instance, it might be helpful for parents to keep in mind that if they notice that their child is becoming reluctant to go to school, this attitude might not only be due to their experiencing difficulties or 'laziness' in relation to their school work, but also perhaps to some incidence of bullying. The more this problem can be talked about openly, the better. What sometimes makes it so difficult and painful for adolescents to broach this issue is that they may feel terribly vulnerable and hurt and their self-esteem may have been damaged. Your support and understanding may be enough to help them get over this crisis. If this is not the case, it is important to liaise with the school and find out whether they can provide a way to deal with the problem. Some schools have set up schemes to address incidents of bullying; in others you (and your adolescent) might need to talk personally with the relevant school authorities.

(An example of the effects of serious bullying that went unnoticed can be found in Chapter 5.)

CHAPTER FOUR

FRIENDSHIP AND SOCIAL LIFE

It is important for teenagers to be able to develop friendships and activities outside the circle of family life. Their development and their sense of identity will depend to some extent on their ability to reach out to new relationships beyond the familiar world of family without, however, losing touch with home as a base.

The parents of fifteen-to-seventeen year old adolescents will be faced with the difficult and often painful task of having to relinquish a degree of control to allow adolescents this new free-dom. It may feel painful to 'let go' at this age for various reasons. Parents may rightly feel that because of immaturity, their teenager is not ready to take on greater freedom and make good use of it. It can also be very painful to be faced with an adolescent for whom you are no longer the centre of the world, and for whom friends and their particular way of life are becoming increasingly influential. In such circumstances, when experiencing teenagers' tendency to turn away and throw themselves into their new world, many parents find it difficult to remember how much their children still need their concern and understanding.

Close friends

Full of emotions, doubts, longings and contradictory feelings, teenagers have a great need to communicate and share with their age group. At this age, teenagers often form an intense friendship with someone who is felt to be very similar to themselves. With this special friend, they can share all their sorrow, hurt, pain, worries and crushes. This friendship may have existed before, but at this time a 'bosom' friend may be invested with a particular intensity. With this friend, teenagers feel they can share absolutely everything and be implicitly understood. This is the time of very long phone calls, where every single little incident of emotional life is related and shared. Often, this closeness with a friend seems to replace an earlier closeness with one of the parents.

For example, as far as Barbara could remember, she had always had a best friend. At primary school she'd been inseparable from her companion and had seen her regularly after school, at weekends, during holidays. At sixteen, she became extremely close to her friend Cathy, with whom she shared her most intimate secrets, fantasies, desires, interests and disappointments. They not only helped each other with homework and any other difficulties they had to face, but they seemed to confide in and trust in each other more than anyone else. They exasperated their respective families with endless telephone calls at all hours of the day and night, usually after they had already spent long hours together. When Barbara found out that Cathy and her family were moving to another town, she felt panic-stricken and depressed. The loss of her best friend was experienced as a real tragedy and it took quite a long time to overcome this ordeal. For many months, she clung desperately to her friend by writing lengthy letters to her. Even this daily exchange of letters could not fill the void that the absence of her friend had left, and so Barbara also continued to phone her regularly, seemingly oblivious not only to the financial burden, but also to the inconvenience of monopolising the phone. As time passed Barbara became aware that the 'adventures' and life style described by Cathy were increasingly different from her own interests. Gradually, the exchanges between the two friends became less frequent and lengthy, although they stayed in contact and remained friends. Barbara grew away from Cathy and eventually became more independent of her.

Groups

Many adolescents spend much of their time alone, locked in their room, reading, day-dreaming, watching TV, playing computer games or listening to music for long periods. They may worry about venturing outside their room and their daydreams because they fear rejection and feel self-conscious. At times, when they seem 'hooked' to their 'Walkman', music seems to function as the key to a solitary, sensual dream world in which adolescents lose themselves.

Becoming a member of a group may help to diffuse such individual anxieties. The group as a whole may perform a containing function for the teenager's emotions and anxieties. Often the group itself contains many different characters which seem to represent the different parts of the teenager's personality. There may be Dennis the lazy one, Sylvia the wild one, Robert, cut off in his own world, and many others. The members of the group usually share some interests: clothes-style, hair, music, sports, idols. The mood of the group may swing from passivity, listening to music in an atmosphere full of smoke and drink, to one of electrical energy.

Adolescents are often passionate about music: they may spend hours listening to their favourite music, playing in bands, 'hanging out' together, or perhaps going to nightclubs. Adolescent boys in particular can become obsessed by fast cars and motorbikes which may embody their desire for power and masculinity. Like many teenagers' preoccupations this has much to do with longing for what is forbidden, either because it is dangerous or because it is an exclusively 'grown-up' activity.

Tony expresses vividly how his group gives him a sense of safety and of some superiority:

"My best friend's parents have an empty basement in their house, so we go to hang out there after school. We moved a couch and a stereo in there and all kinds of junk. Lots of kids come round to chat with us: our mates, of course, but also guys who live on the street and other people from school. And girls – we like to have lots of girls down there. In the beginning, we couldn't get that many girls to come, but then we got this reputation of being a wild bunch. That brought them pretty fast. Not that we really tried to do wild things, we're just good at getting stupid ideas and convincing other kids to help us. We're the leaders of the group, especially my best friend; he enjoys bossing people around. I don't mind doing what he says as long as it sounds fun. Anyway, I'm the one who gets most of the ideas. I'm the one who thinks about how to get things moving, but my friend is better at convincing others.

There's six of us at the core of the gang, and lots of other kids who try hard to be like us. Some of them are all right. It's just that we don't try to be anything, we just are, so the other kids sometimes have a hard time following. My friend likes to watch them try, though. I sometimes resent it. It's like having a bunch of copycats monkeying around you.

The six of us get along very well. We're all really different and sometimes we wonder what we see in one another. Somebody to talk to, I suppose. Most of us can't speak of our lives to our parents. They wouldn't understand and we'd have to lie, so why bother? But we can talk to each other. We like to think of ourselves as a family. When we're close together, nobody can touch us, no one ever dares to come near. And it really helps with the girls."

Belonging to a group allows adolescents to distance themselves enough from their family to discover a world of their own. On the other hand, most groups place immense pressure on the adolescent to conform and it can be worrying for parents to see that their teenager is unable to resist the group's influence. Ultimately, we all hope that adolescents will acquire the strength and sense of individual identity to form their own values and judgements.

Pressure to conform

Because of their uncertain sense of identity and their insecurity about themselves, some adolescents may feel pushed into doing things they may not otherwise feel comfortable about. They may pretend to be 'cool' or 'tough' in order to be noticed and accepted by the group. The following description by seventeen year old Anna tells about the security of belonging to the group, but also the fear of falling out with it and the unspoken pressures to have sex without really wanting to do so. "The group gives you a structure, you always know who is going to ring you, the way of doing things, where you will go and what you will do on Saturday night. You feel safe in one way because you can't be touched when you are in a group. But it is terrifying to think you might be pushed out. There are core members who can't be touched and the 'hangers on' who are treated badly, but always hope to 'get in'. If you don't have a boyfriend that you are sleeping with, you are made to feel that you are missing out. The other girls talk among themselves about what they've done and they say you are just a baby, you wouldn't understand. It hurts when they say that. It is a mystery you feel excluded from."

The outsider

Sean, sixteen, isn't allowed by his parents to go out at night with his group of friends. Therefore he feels he doesn't quite belong. He says: "I'm an outsider and I have developed an image as an eccentric. As an outsider at my age, you can either be ridiculed and mocked as a sissy and 'square', or you can be treated as something of an eccentric, and this is what I'm trying to do. But I still play a role. I feel I need to adopt the role of someone who doesn't worry about what people think of me. It is then a stance that you have to maintain, retaining a reserve, a distance from people, not allowing people to read you. The people in that group boast about girls and getting stoned, but they don't have a strong sense of identity outside the group activity. They boast about girls but they are afraid of any emotional commitment. I am strong enough not to flaunt my clothes or my physique, but I do body-building and I am proud of myself."

In the example of Sean, one can see how a sensitive and intelligent adolescent managed to preserve his dignity despite his exclusion from the mainstream of the group. He also tells us, though, what it costs him, and how he has to hide his feelings for fear of showing how much he really cares about the group. As parents, you may have noticed your adolescent dressing and behaving in an eccentric way. Although their appearance and behaviour may be provocative, it may be a desperate attempt, as the example of Sean shows, to gain all-important recognition from their age-group.

Going out, drinking

An increasing number of teenagers think of fun and entertainment in terms of going out on Saturday night to the pub, a party, a club and getting drunk. Many teenagers feel that by drinking, they show their coolness or toughness and will be accepted as 'one of the lads' in the group. Deep down, they often feel that they can't face their fears of loneliness, of not being socially, physically and sexually adequate, and the exclusion from the group. They try to escape from these fears by mindless drinking or drugs. Adolescents need a lot of inner strength to tolerate these anxieties. Julian, for example, described the excitement and the highs and lows of going out to a party on Saturday night and meeting a girl. "I went out on Saturday night to a nightclub. It takes your mind off things, makes you feel you do something. You shake around and dance, you go with the music, the lights and the smoke. Everybody is drinking. If you don't drink, it makes you self-aware and you want to relax with loud music, you want to enjoy it like everybody else, you want to be 'in' with the people laughing. There was this girl, really nice. I sat next to her and we talked a bit. I was drinking. I had to go to the toilet and left her for a moment. She might have thought that I had just left her. When I came back she was talking with another boy. He was a DJ – they all worship him. He has got a car and money. I just stood there, all awkward. I just wanted to go home then. I wasn't having a good time any more." Obviously, Julian was longing to forget himself. He throws himself into drinking and dancing and feels very happy when he can make contact with a nice girl. However, his 'high' is precarious. When it doesn't work out, he is forlorn and depressed.

Soft drugs

Taking hash or marijuana, getting stoned, being 'spaced out', can be part of the ethos of some groups. As with drinking, the aim may be to get rid of inhibitions and bring about an artificial sense of well-being. But the effects can be quite unpredictable and, far from the 'desired high', teenagers may experience much darker moods and a sense of being helplessly cut off from themselves and others. Julian, whom we mentioned earlier, gave this account, describing people at a party: "I went upstairs and everybody there was stoned, in a dark room, not socialising, locking themselves away. They are hiding, they don't want to think or to talk to anybody else. They try to be someone else, they try to be 'cool'."

Although many young people may experiment with soft drugs without, however, getting 'hooked', some can become psychologically dependent on hash or marijuana. They start by taking a joint on Saturday nights, then gradually need to have some every day because they can't face the day or night without it.

CHAPTER FIVE

WHEN THINGS GO WRONG

This chapter will look at some of the more serious disorders that can arise in adolescence. We appreciate that many parents, as well as teenagers, are very anxious about issues such as hard drugs, eating disorders and suicide attempts. We hope that the following examples will be a help in promoting dialogue between you and your teenager if a serious problem is developing. In all the examples given, the problem was very much worsened by domestic crises and a subsequent sense of isolation on the part of the young people concerned, and this is the part that can be avoided.

Hard drugs

We all know the very harmful effects of hard drugs. We know that they ruin people's lives both physically and mentally. Not everyone who uses drugs is an addict, but people can gradually become dependent on drugs without knowing it. Emma, for example, described her own battle with drugs over a number of years. Eventually she managed to overcome it with the help of counselling. She is now happily married with a little baby. At sixteen, she remembered being bright, outgoing, coping very well at school. Then she fell in with the wrong crowd, started taking drugs and got addicted to them. Her father, whom she was very close to, died and her mother married again, to a man Emma disliked.

Emma wrote an account of her experience: "Hard drugs were known by all of us to constitute an inevitable escalation towards drug-dependency and abuse; they also showed that you had 'fallen in with the wrong crowd' and by the age of seventeen, I had done just that. If anything, this should have been proved to me by an incident which occurred early on in my relationship with this new group of friends, in the course of which I was invited with them to what was described as a birthday party. Someone had taken a lot of time over the party preparations! Without my being aware of it, I took hashish (the birthday cake), mescalin (the jam-like icing which everyone was generously spreading on the cake) and marijuana: a colourful cocktail invented for the happy circumstances! I spent the next few days recovering from hallucinations under the surprised gaze of my mother, who seemed concerned that I had managed to get such a hangover from a little excessive drinking at a party. I concluded that although still angry for not having been forewarned about the various ingredients involved in the celebration, I was in with a 'fun', artistic and intelligent crowd, all slightly hippyish and inventive, and drugs were not the dangerous, downward, life-draining forces they were thought to be. Indeed, when 'taken properly' for the sole purpose of having fun and being with friends, they were certainly something one could master. They were a recreational tool just like drinks for the older crowd. Besides, none of my friends had the look of a junkie. In fact, in retrospect I realise that they were really, most of them, 'druggies', that is, someone hooked but not terminally wasted. Nothing to worry about, we were all a happy bunch having fun, the world belonged to us. If every now and then we lacked the stamina to enjoy it to its fullest extent (that is, being able to stay up all night partying and survive the next day), it turned out there was always some nice 'friend' (dealer, disguised as some nice young guy) on hand anywhere we went, to provide us with harder drugs. Some two years of off-and-on abuse led me finally to the 'miraculous' properties of hard drugs. But the main pattern of my relationship to drugs had been set by the initial group experiences and the thought that even hard drugs could be mastered to suit one's purposes. In fact drugs began to seem appropriate under any circumstances, recreational or not. The illegal drugs were easy to get hold of given the surprising number of 'dealer friends' there were everywhere, not just among the 'nightclubbies'. By then, at eighteen, I had tried a great number of mood enhancers, be they legal or illegal: it didn't matter, as long as I had what it took to function without the slightest loss of energy (and without anyone noticing my quiet addiction) in the day time and sleep without remembering at night."

To have to witness your own adolescent not only slipping away from the family, but being taken over by such a self-destructive way of life is every parent's nightmare. As with other problems we have mentioned, the first step may be to try to talk with your adolescent about what you see happening to them and attempt to regain parental authority while, if possible, talking to them and encouraging them to be more responsible for themselves. If the situation proves to be intractable, do not hesitate to seek professional help and support for your adolescent. It may also be helpful for you to get some specialist advice on how best to deal with the problem. A number of helpful organisations are listed at the back of this book.

Gangs and anti-social groups

Some teenage groups have a predominantly violent basis; they are more like 'gangs'. They are not just 'defiant' in an adolescent kind of way, but they get involved in anti-social, delinquent acts, such as taking and dealing in hard drugs, vandalism, stealing and violence, etc. In fact, 'anti' defines what these gangs are about: out to attack growth, development and hope. To belong to this kind of gang, the members have to do violence to the vulnerable, sensitive aspect of their own personality. Deep grievances, often stemming from childhood and a wish for revenge against parental figures, seem to motivate the members of the gang. It may happen that an adolescent, driven to carry on with anti-social acts, falls deeper and deeper into cynicism when in fact, he may wish to stop and escape from the grip of the gang. This may be extremely difficult because 'mafia-like' ringleaders promise an illusion of protection to their members. At a deeper level, the anti-social group promises protection against the pain of growing up and awareness of any emotional life.

Emma's 'group' in the example above in fact turned out to be a 'gang'. The older members who were throwing the birthday party, already on drugs themselves, took cynical pleasure in corrupting the younger people. Although initially angry about having been manipulated and tricked, Emma gradually made the values of the gang her own and succumbed to the world of drugs. She felt that she could then escape from the pain of her father's death, and her feelings of rage and betrayal about her mother's quick remarriage to a stepfather she deeply resented. But the state of euphoria and excitement induced by the drugs was followed by deep depression. Emma left her studies, becoming completely dependent on drugs to cope with the outside world. Perhaps, had she been able at an earlier time to talk with her mother and share the traumatic events that affected their lives, she wouldn't have had to wait until her early twenties when, with the help of a boyfriend, she looked for professional help, and managed with great difficulty to pull herself out of the grip of the gang and drugs.

Eating disorders

Teenagers can not only have food fads, they can also be extremely variable in their eating habits: at times they may indulge excessively in food and at other times they may seem completely uninterested. These adolescent variations differ from serious eating disorders which can occur.

A growing number of teenagers, girls in particular, suffer from eating disorders. In the conditions of bulimia or anorexia, there is an overwhelming obsession with food: organising meals, eating huge amounts of food or thinking of how to manage not to eat while at the same time pretending to do so. The function of food, which is originally life-sustaining and represents the proto-type of a nourishing relationship, can acquire other attributes. For bulimics, food is used as a comfort, as a way of filling a sense of emptiness, or perhaps a response to a feeling of self-loathing. Usually, a binge is followed by self-disgust, a wish to punish oneself, and by vomiting, to stay slim. In fact the need to stay slim seems to be an obsession for most girls with eating disorders. Girls are constantly bombarded with fashion images in the media, pro-moting the waif-like, ethereal, skinny body. Most adolescents are self-conscious and very unhappy and critical about the shape of their bodies, which are far from the 'perfect' image they are confronted with and aspire to. They are led to believe that posses-sion of this idealised body will be the key to acceptability, happi-ness, love and success. So it is not surprising that when they feel they have to get into a bathing suit or to go to an important party, they might put themselves on a very strict diet. This can be the beginning of a downward spiral in which the adolescent wants to lose more and more weight. They usually don't see this extreme loss as a problem, as they have a very distorted view of their bodies. Often, girls with eating disorders cannot cope with the feelings and emotions evoked by the upheavals of adolescence. They find them unmanageable and try to avoid them by controlling and managing their own body. Eating disorders can be life-threatening. It is important to recognise the signs as early as possible should you notice that your adolescent girl is losing too much weight or becoming obsessed with dieting.

Judith, for instance, had been independent since she was little and had always been considered an ambitious girl who coped well. When she was eighteen months old, her younger brother was born suffering from congenital disease and needing several operations. For a while, Judith's parents doubted that he would survive. Judith became depressed, as she experienced her mother as emotionally unavailable to her but soon recovered, stopped being demanding and started happily at nursery school. At fifteen, she was an attractive, popular and bright girl, excelling in academic work and sports, very competitive, bright and hard working. She started going out with a boy who once pointed out light-heartedly that she was a little 'podgy'. Judith instantly decided to go on a diet and become slim like her best friend. After a few weeks she was extremely pleased to see that she had lost weight and decided to lose some more. Gradually she couldn't stop herself dieting any more. Counting calories and losing weight became a kind of drug. This obsessive dieting was kept secret from her family, and to some extent from herself, as she didn't acknowledge that there was any problem. She gradually lost interest in anything but food and how to avoid it. She felt in 'total control' except for moments when she would feel depressed and feared 'she was going crazy'. She started leading a double life. She coped cheerfully on the outside but was full of lies and deceit and endless calculations and manipulations, very unlike the way she used to be.

Aware that her mother had started to worry about her, but that both her parents were too busy at work and perhaps not wanting to face the truth about the course of her illness, Judith found a way of pretending to eat at the family evening meal, which later on would be vomited out. Alternatively, calories would be lost by doing some carefully planned jogging. Whenever her mother became anxious and confronted her about her loss of weight, Judith reassured her that she was in control and was eating perfectly all right. If she was ever worried about her compulsive habit, her loss of weight and her growing weakness, anxieties would dissipate when she looked at herself in the mirror. Though extremely skinny by this time, she would see her body as 'obscenely fat'. Her performance at her school work had started to deteriorate. Judith began to find it difficult to concentrate. Eventually she confided in a friend who, very alarmed, talked to a teacher and it was one of the school staff who eventually rang Judith's parents over their concern about Judith. Judith's parents by this time had become very alarmed by her state but no amount of exhortation, nagging or even the threat of being deprived of holidays, seemed to make any difference. She wouldn't stop starving herself. Beside herself with worry, Judith's mother referred her to a psychiatrist specialising in the treatment of eating disorders. Judith was referred to a Unit for anorexics. They provided individual psychotherapy for her and parental counselling for her parents. After six weeks she was able to leave the Unit because her parents were able to help her at home with her eating difficulties. But she and her parents carried on with their regular sessions at the Unit, looking at the issues underlying the eating difficulties.

Since early childhood, Judith had always been a coping, independent, self-reliant girl. When her little brother was born and her parents' anxieties about his survival took their whole attention away from her, she didn't really express her jealousy, her rage and her pain. Feelings were never acknowledged and worked through. Her personality seemed to be built on being in control, being a high flier, without really being in touch with her feelings. Judith seemed to have become very scared, feeling overwhelmed by anxieties related to adolescence, to begin being 'a woman' with the pressures to be 'beautiful and slim'. She became obsessed by a wish to control her body, but the obsessions took control of her and her life. Judith's parents couldn't notice what was going on for a long time, perhaps because they couldn't bear to think that their brilliant girl had become a very ill girl.

Suicide attempts

Suicide attempts in young adolescents may stem from an underlying sense of isolation, worthlessness and depression, but often tend to be impulsive acts, triggered by something which to the outsider might seem quite trivial. They are often a call for attention. It may be a fight or a misunderstanding, a problem at school or a break-up with a friend which leads to feelings of hopelessness, rage and despair.

Howard was a very shy and sensitive fifteen year old. His parents split up when he was four years old. His mother remarried when he was ten, but she and her new partner did not get on well and Howard witnessed a lot of fights. Howard's mother, although concerned about her son, was very taken up by her work and personal life. She was close to him when he was a little boy but had found it difficult to notice the subtle ways in which he had begun to change and develop in recent years. Because she was out of touch with the adolescent that he had become (though his secretive manner certainly didn't help her to reach him) their relationship was no longer a close and understanding one. Howard and his stepfather had also become quite distant from one another. In particular he resented his stepfather's heavy drinking and recriminations against his mother. Howard became a lonely adolescent, spending long hours day-dreaming in his room. He had a great passion for the cinema, especially for old American classic movies. His pocket money would go on trips to the cinema with Robert, his only friend. Sometimes he would attempt to compose film scripts, dream for hours of either acting in or directing them, but then would despair that his gangly and awkward physique in no way resembled that of his hero, Marlon Brando. Sexually, he felt confused, not quite sure whether he was more attracted to women or to men. He was very ashamed of this dark secret and found it difficult to talk about. At school, he kept to himself, not belonging to any group. In fact there was a group of boys in his class who belittled others by name-calling. They made fun of Howard and called him a 'poof' several times because he hated the rough games the others engaged in. He felt very hurt and full of rage, and became reluctant to go to school. Increasingly, his mother had to spend a long time getting him out of bed. One day, she got extremely irritated with him, worrying about being late for her work. She shouted at him telling him he was a good-for-nothing like his father. After his mother and stepfather had left for work, Howard was left alone at home. He felt "there was no point in life" and was full of self-loathing and dislike for his mother, stepfather and the school, who all seemed to confirm his sense of worthlessness. He took fifty paracetamol. Later that day, his mother found him and immediately sought appropriate help.

In this case, as in most suicide attempts, Howard's desperate action was an attempt to draw attention to his plight. For Howard, the attempt on his life did put him in touch with someone who could listen and think with him about the long downward spiral which had finally led to the attempt on his own life.

A suicidal gesture may never be repeated, but it should nevertheless always be taken seriously and its causes explored by professionals. Should an adolescent repeatedly attempt to put his life at risk, this would be a clear indication that professional help is needed very urgently.

CHAPTER SIX

THE TEENAGER AND SEXUALITY

The metamorphosis of the body

The uniqueness of each adolescent's maturing body may provoke a lot of anxiety. Adolescents ask themselves a lot of questions about their bodies: Is it normal? Is it properly masculine or properly feminine? Is it too fat or too thin? Is it attractive? Is it developing and maturing fast enough? How does it compare with others?

At times these questions seem so pressing that adolescents feel quite overwhelmed by them. They become strangers to themselves. They may feel at the mercy of bodily changes which seem to take place despite themselves. At times, they may feel proud of these changes and like spending hours on end gazing at their reflection in the mirror, scrutinizing and admiring what they see. However, more often than not, the image that they encounter falls short of what they would like to be.

Teenagers are sometimes haunted and tormented by the slightest imperfection on their face. They may well feel that a blemish (like a spot) will be seen by the whole world, proving that something is deeply wrong with their body, and therefore with their whole person. Caroline, for example, is a pretty sixteen-year-old adolescent. She cries her eyes out and pushes her family to despair when she has a few spots on her face. She refuses to go out of the house in spite of her mother pleading with her to do so. There seems to be a deeply critical voice inside Caroline telling her that if she isn't perfect, it is better not to put in an appearance at all. The spot, which she feels is spoiling her face, expresses the fear that if she isn't perfect, without blemish, she must be rubbish with something monstrous in her which is unbearable to her as well as to everyone else.

Whereas Caroline cannot bear the reflection she meets of herself in the mirror and a pimple takes dramatic proportions, another girl, Juliette tried to escape a negative image of herself by fantasising that a photographer with access to the most beautiful women in the world, would fall for her rather than any of his models. At seventeen, Juliette, for example, looking back and reflecting on how she felt at the age of fifteen, said: "At fifteen I had these long, very secret passions for older boys that I was too shy to do anything about. But my dream was to go out with a much older man who would be a photographer from the arty, fashionable world and introduce me to the world of nightclubs and models. I wanted to be right on the inside of that world, one up on my old friends." Juliette was in fact insecure about her own physical appearance and her own identity. She felt that the only way to assert herself was to be one up on the other girls. She wanted to be the most beautiful and fashionable of all her friends. She dreamt of being chosen by a fashion photographer because of her beauty. While Juliette was going through this period, her parents often found her irritating, full of diffidence, but also competitiveness and arrogance. At seventeen, Juliette seemed to be more confident and less self-absorbed. She had made friends and developed interests which were no longer centred on the importance of her appearance and its effect on friends of her own age.

This typical worry about the adolescents' appearance in comparison to the rest of their age group was very evident in Jack. Jack, fifteen, was convinced that he was the only one in his class who had been circumcised. He very much enjoyed games but had to work out a whole series of elaborate excuses for not taking a shower after them. He would sit himself on a bench near the showers, hidden from the other boys, and from this position would inspect them to see whether any of them had been circumcised so as to decide whether he could afford to have a shower himself. In Jack, one can see the shame and shyness that some adolescents experience when they feel themselves to be different from the rest of their age group. Concern about showing their genitals in particular, and exposing themselves to the possible ridicule of their friends, can lead to anxieties about school games or swimming.

Sexual curiosity

Emily, at seventeen, remembered earlier years. "At fifteen my main preoccupation was to be loved by everyone. I thought I was very ugly. I would refuse to go out partly because I felt too ugly, but at the same time I would get very sorry for myself. Very often I would over-react. I would be stuck in my own fears although deep down, I thought I wasn't really that ugly. I didn't like fifteen-year-old boys; they were hot and sticky and smelly, always trying to kiss you. I was excited by men, curious and very flattered and scared when they looked at me. My major preoccupation was sexual. Having sex would be a way of knowing what it is to be a woman. The secrets of the adult world would be revealed to me. At the end of my sixteenth year, I fell in love with John and I asked him to sleep with me. I was incredibly curious. When we did have sex, I didn't feel anything. I then later went up to my mother's bed and I slept there. I felt that I needed to be near her."

Emily's account gives us some hints about the complexity of feeling and fantasies which may underlie an adolescent's forays into the world of adult sexuality. Her wish to sleep with John may have been partially motivated by a very early need to be loved and accepted, despite what she perceived as her ugliness, as well as by a fascination with the mysterious, locked adult world, the only key to which seemed to be the ritual act of losing her virginity. However, she then needed to spend a night in her mother's bed, seeking as a frightened child, warmth, safety and comfort from her mother.

Masturbation

It is common for many adolescents to masturbate. Masturbation can bring relief from pent up sexual excitement and urges. It is often accompanied by fantasies of sexual encounters with partners of their choice and a kind of childish omnipotence may dominate these fantasies. Masturbation accompanied by these exciting intense fantasies may in some cases be followed by a feeling of confusion or depression. However, the fantasies may also be of a more comforting and tender kind. It seems that perhaps boys more frequently than girls experience the feeling of being possessed by aggressive sexual urges.

Falling in love

When adolescents fall in love, they are often so deeply moved by the intensity of their feelings that they may stop sleeping, eating or concentrating on anything else. In their day-dreams, they may imagine situations, different scenarios, in which they are reunited with their loved one. The adolescent brings all his fantasies and longings to this new relationship. An intense need to recover an idealised object, often the mother of early childhood with whom the child felt or longed to be in perfect union, is expressed. There is a search for wholeness, beauty, a longing for someone who understands without words, who supports and will accept completely. This longing for a paradise lost never completely vanishes. However, the overwhelming intensity of these feelings in adolescents can be worrying and frightening, not only for the family, but for themselves, because it seems to swallow up all their energy and take over their lives. When the relationship between two young people can be developed beyond the crush stage, they can begin to try to get to know each other as real people with genuine feelings and needs.

Sally, sixteen, was a quiet, attractive girl but deep down, she felt quite diffident about herself. She was very attached to her father who, however, left the family to live with a young woman when Sally was fourteen. She met Robert at a youth organisation and they fell in love. She thought that he was wonderful – tall, good-looking, a nice person to be with, and she felt he would protect her. A few months later, he left for university in another town. Sally was very upset and worried that he would fall in love with another girl. They wrote letters and spoke on the phone each week. Then on the phone, Robert mentioned a girl who was doing the same course as him, and with whom he was studying. In answer to Sally's very suspicious and alarmed questions, Robert reassured her that she was just a student friend, and anyway, that she had a boyfriend. In her panic, Sally simply could not believe him. In her mind's eye, she saw all her fears of being betrayed confirmed, and believed that he had stopped loving her. To her mother and her younger sister's great alarm, she took to bed, said she was ill and wept for days. She had always been a conscientious student, but now declared she wasn't interested in her studies any more. She said she had lost all interest. Continuous phone calls from Robert didn't lift her spirits. However, when at the end of term, Robert came back home on holiday and they met again, she realised that his feelings for her had not changed, and that a false scenario had been created in her own mind. For the first time, they really talked about their feelings for each other, and what separation had meant to them. Robert admitted that he felt jealous about a relationship that Sally had with a boy in her form. When he had to go back to university, they both cried and shared their feelings of insecurity and fear of whether they could be faithful and wait for each other. They could begin to trust each other because they had dared to show each other their vulnerable sides and thus, have less idealised images of each other.

Homosexuality

As we have seen, adolescence is a volatile and passionate time. Teenagers are drawn to different people and ideas. This is as true of sexual matters as it is of other issues discussed in this book. It is important to remember this when trying to resist the pressure of labelling your adolescent even when you find yourself confronted with the 'fact' of their being homosexual ('gay' or 'lesbian'). It is not infrequent for young adolescents to feel sexually aroused in the presence of a person of the same sex. They may or may not act upon this attraction but this experience can evoke quite confusing and disturbing feelings. In places such as single-sex boarding schools where casual encounters with the opposite sex are rare, this sort of situation is even more likely to occur. More often than not, this experience will not have a lasting effect on their sexual identity or choice of future partners. However, some will discover that they continue to prefer partners of the same gender. Whatever your personal feelings or reactions, if your adolescent 'comes out' and makes this known to you or gives reason to believe that this is what is happening, your sympathetic understanding of their turmoil can only be helpful to them.

Break-up and break-down in relationships

When a romantic relationship breaks up or when feelings are not returned, adolescents sometimes fall into an abyss of despair and anger. The feeling is that life is over, that they will never love or be loved again, expressing in this way their deepest fear, namely that they are not lovable, not good enough. The break-up revives childhood fears and jealousies, times when the child felt excluded or unwanted by one or the other parent. It is important for us as parents to take these feelings seriously, and to listen and to try to talk. This can be painful because it puts one in touch with one's own disappointments, disillusionments and failed relationships.

Adolescents do have a very dramatic way of making parents feel the intensity of their emotions. In the example given earlier, Sally had expressed her depression by retreating to her bed. It was perhaps a bid for her mother's attention and a concrete expression of her deep need to be looked after at that moment. Her mother's understanding of her need for comfort and reassurance surely helped Sally to bear and integrate the difficult feelings associated with her past loss and present depression.

Contraception

Whatever one's personal convictions, it is important not to believe that teenagers can be controlled by veto. It can be easy to forget that they are growing up in a different environment from parents and therefore have different expectations and pressures. It seems crucial to be able to hold on to an atmosphere in the family which allows issues related to contraception or sexually transmitted diseases to be thought about and discussed in a non-judgemental way. We may feel that our children might have been exposed to this information through sex education programmes and friends and the media. Today, more than ever before, because of the danger of AIDS, it is important that adolescents know how to protect themselves and their partners.

Sophie, for instance, met Ben at a party when she was sixteen and he was twenty-three. Sophie was deeply impressed by his age, assurance and good looks. When they slept together a few weeks later, Ben convinced Sophie that using condoms would ruin the intimacy, and assured her that he would 'be careful'. Sophie, who was not using any other form of birth control because this was her first sexual experience, did not want to ruin what she felt was the big moment of her life with mundane concerns of pregnancy and sexually transmitted diseases.

When Sophie arrived home in the early morning, now feeling a free young woman, she found her parents waiting for her, beside themselves with worry and anger. Her parents shouted at her, because she had neglected to ring. When they heard where she had been they were shaken that their little girl, as she still seemed to them, had taken this step. Her mother asked Sophie if she had used protection: Sophie blithely admitted she hadn't. Her mother screamed and had to hold herself from hitting her. She realised, however, that it was vital that she retain Sophie's trust if Sophie was to confide in her in the future. She took Sophie to the doctor to get advice and help and they were both very reassured when he suggested that Sophie take 'the morning-after pill'. Later, they had a long talk together about contraception and talked over their feelings about what had happened that night.

As this example shows, the whole issue of sexual relationships and contraception is a very loaded one for both teenagers and parents. Not only is it important for teenagers to be convinced about the necessity of protecting themselves, but if their rational resolve does falter in the 'heat of the moment' there should be the trust for them to come freely and talk, however difficult it may be.

Pregnancy

Unplanned pregnancy in adolescents can be accidental, but it is often the result of an unconscious wish to have a baby. This longing for a baby may arise from a wish both to give and receive affection, and this may be particularly acute in adolescents who feel unloved, deprived and inadequate. They may hope that a baby will not only bring love, but also meaning. Through caring for her baby, the teenage girl may feel that she can escape from an awareness of her own feelings of vulnerability and neediness, and from life's struggles. By nursing her baby, she may also be mothering her own baby self inside the baby. Teenage girls with very young mothers often get pregnant at the same age as when their mother had their first baby.

It is very important for a pregnant adolescent girl to be given the opportunity to make up her own mind as to whether or not to keep the baby. She may need help and support in trying to make this difficult decision, in exploring her real wishes and conflicts and whether she feels capable or not of looking after a baby. Were adolescent girls and boys more informed about the needs of a real baby, they might develop a more thoughtful and responsible attitude towards pregnancy. In our opinion, it is essential that the school curriculum should deal in some depth with the development of infants and children, as well as principles of parenting.

Pauline was a quiet, reserved, sixteen-year-old girl who had been fostered in her infancy. Unlike a lot of the girls in her year, she didn't particularly go around in gangs or groups. But by the age of sixteen, she became involved with a boy although previously she had been rather shy of boys. Very quickly she became pregnant and was determined to have the baby. Her foster mother was very sensitive to her wish to hold on to the baby, though she was disappointed and in many ways concerned that Pauline was pregnant at too young an age. She supported Pauline in a way that enabled her to be a mother and to continue with her studies.

In this particular case, Pauline's resolve to keep and look after her baby may perhaps be understood as a wish to give her child a beginning in life that she had never had herself.

Abortion

When an adolescent decides to terminate her pregnancy and opt for an abortion, she may experience a whole range of different emotions. Some girls may feel relieved whereas others may be burdened with a sense of guilt, regret and depression. More often than not, they may go through a mixture of all these different emotions, and it is important that they feel supported and understood during this distressing period. Where a girl feels so guilty about having aborted her baby that she is left with a sense of lingering depression counselling should be sought; others may not feel that the experience was so traumatic and may be able to put it behind them.

Frequent changes of sexual partners or promiscuity

It is quite common for adolescents to change partners frequently; this might be part of the life-style of their friends and due to the pressures from the 'group'. The quest for novelty may be part of an exciting, wild experimentation with life and sexuality. Through these frequent changes of partners, teenagers may also be expressing a fear of closeness and involvement. They may also be showing their need to be in control: they are going to change or drop partners when they feel like it, not the other way round.

When promiscuity is compulsive, it may signal that the teenager is acting out some underlying anxieties or conflict with their parents. Teenagers may in fact be saying something like: "When I was little, you were having all the fun and I was helplessly excluded. Now it's my turn and you can't stop me."

Alice, sixteen, was describing to her older cousin aged

twenty three, what she called her sexual freedom, which is something she carefully keeps away from her parents. "On Saturday night, I get drunk at nightclubs and sleep with blokes. It is not a big deal having sex, I don't feel emotional about the man I am having a relationship with. I like to feel the excitement." Although Alice was speaking in a defiant way, underneath she was quite worried about her recklessness and wanted someone to help her to stop it. She added later that she didn't sleep well at night. Since she was little, she had needed to have the light on at night, and she frequently had to go to her parents' bedroom for reassurance. She felt anxious, and had nightmares about a sudden death. Alice found it relatively easy to talk to her cousin who she thought was wiser than her, but at the same time, was not an authority figure. It became clear in these discussions that as well as a promiscuous teenager, there was a little child, lonely, uncontained, scared to die and yet angry with her parents for what she saw as their neglect of her. 'Living dangerously' was used like a drug to escape from these fears which could be traced back to early childhood. The sense that Alice was putting herself at risk physically and emotionally alarmed her cousin, who finally managed to persuade her to speak to her mother about what she was doing.

CHAPTER SEVEN

COPING WITH SOCIETY

The World Stage

It is small wonder, given the tumultuous emotional and physical changes taking place within teenagers, that at times they wish to effect changes themselves. A wider stage can be used to bring about such changes and to express their own personalities. They can fight with passion and raw energy for the things they believe in, often aimed at making the world a better place to be. Interest in ecology and human rights are good examples. Other causes chosen could express a rebellion against authority based on conflicts unresolved within the family. Rather than replicate the old arguments within a family setting, many teenagers succeed in finding other groups within which they can freely express their points of view. Involvement in organisations can also provide a structure that may be lacking at home. The following examples will provide different perspectives.

Lisa became very involved in a youth movement which held international meetings. She spoke glowingly to her relatives of the importance of international friendship and of breaking down cultural barriers. Her parents were amazed. Was this the same Lisa who would lie in bed during the weekend with barely a civil word to say either to them or her brother? It is an important question and one which must puzzle teenagers and parents alike. How is it that the gregarious pursuit of international co-operation and friendship can take place alongside sulkiness or non-co-operation at home? Is it merely hypocrisy, wanting to present a good front to hide the reality? That would be a harsh judgement on a complex picture. Perhaps it is better thought of in terms of two different sides of the same coin - an attempt to be co-operative and finding this possible only outside the dynamics of the family. Initially some adolescents need the help of groups and organisations to give expression to the generous side of their nature.

Involvement in a cause can provide the necessary space within which healing can take place. Bob, for example, was seventeen, one of two children in a close family where both parents were much involved in family life. Recently his sister, Lucie, had begun to complain of dizziness and headaches. Quite quickly she had lost her appetite and weight and generally looked quite ill. For some time, exhaustive medical tests were required. It was a tremendously anxious time for all the family and had a profound impact on Bob.

Lucie was determinedly cheerful and optimistic, but Bob was extremely distressed at how she had changed, particularly in her looks. He was by nature a solitary person, performing competently in studies without really seeming to commit himself thoroughly. The clarinet, particularly jazz music, seemed to be his first love. During his sister's illness he increasingly withdrew from social situations, concentrating only on his music. He became an excellent musician but his isolation worried his parents. They had tried to talk to Bob about his sister, but he had never been communicative at the best of times. He was considerate to his sister in practical ways and would push her to some functions in the wheelchair that she had come to need. He found it difficult to talk to her with any degree of spontaneity. It was his music that provided the opportunity to do more. He was persuaded to join a small group of other jazz enthusiasts. At first, this new group seemed to turn inwards on itself and, if anything, this inwardness increased his parents' anxiety. But as they improved and developed an identity as a group they beganto attract a small following. Bob seemed to find his voice and suggested that they give performances. It is hard to know whether it was intentional or not, but he made several contacts and became involved with groups specialising in work with children and adults who had communication problems. Although his sister's illness obviously had an important impact on him, perhaps his own reaction to that illness, a reaction which left him without words, led him to a deeper appreciation of the frustration of not being able to communicate in words and to the emergence of his communication through music.

Angry causes

John began to worry his parents very much as he approached seventeen. He had moved from one enthusiasm to the next for some years. He had, for example, been a keen collector of stamps, had then been very involved in model-making of different kinds and had recently become interested in outdoor activities such as hiking and camping. When involved in the latest interest, he would become absorbed in it, and would withdraw, quite happily apparently, from the hurly-burly of family life. Recently this tendency to be part of the family and yet to be detached from it had undergone a change which had seemingly appeared overnight. John began to give voice to strong opinions on family matters. His father liked to go fishing when he had some free time, although it was a family joke that they would have starved long ago if they had relied on his endeavours for their food. To John, however, his father's liking for fishing was incomprehensible. How could he knowingly cause pain to harmless animals that did him no harm? The arguments that developed as soon as the fishing tackle appeared in the hallway had become more and more heated and increasingly, John's mother, Mary, felt plunged into the middle of a conflict between John and his father. It was clear that unlike earlier pursuits, John was persevering with his commitment to animal rights. Nonetheless, it was a shock to hear from him that he had been cautioned by the police for his role in sabotaging a foxhunt. It turned out that there had been a fracas at the convening point of the hunt. Although he was embarrassed by how far he had gone, he also obviously got much pleasure from his activities. Furthermore, when he managed to describe his enjoyment, it became clear that running across fields and laying false trails for the hounds combined his love of the open air and a thrill for the chase. These elements had much in common with his father's liking for the open air and angling, even though John's motive was to hunt the hunters rather than the fish.

A time for idealism

It can be seen from the above examples that such causes provide an important opportunity for teenagers to give expression to their points of view and to develop an aspect of their personality that can only be given shape in a bigger grouping than that of the family. When teenagers join groups and causes, they become influenced by other members and join in the activities without fully understanding the motivation for what they are doing. It is doubtful, for example, that Lisa would have thought that there was such an obvious contrast between the cheerful availability that characterised her activity in the youth movement, and her sulkiness and unavailability at home. In fact, if she had been able to think too much about the apparent double standards, this might have made it difficult for her to give expression to this generous side of her. The youth movement provided an atmosphere where she didn't feel judged. It also made it possible for her to help to form a better society than the one she helped to create at home, one where young people could interact freely and get along more harmoniously.

Sometimes adolescent causes can be mocked by adults because they transparently represent only one part of an argument, or because they involve a flight from reality. But it would be a mistake not to recognise that the strength of adolescent movements comes precisely from their full-bloodedness and honesty, which is not daunted by the adult wish to compromise. It is this tension between the experience of adults and the youthful, often impatient thrust of adolescence which has been a recurring theme of this book. Change, if it is to happen, only comes about when received wisdom is challenged, however painful the process.

CHAPTER EIGHT

APPROACHING EIGHTEEN

Robin, nearing his eighteenth birthday, reflected with an uncle on the changes that had happened to him over the last three years. He could see that he had changed profoundly but couldn't quite work out how it had happened. It seemed, for example, that his relationships with members of his family had changed. Certainly, he didn't fight with them as much as he had done: at one time it seemed that every attempt to gain greater independence met with resistance. His father, in particular, used to be very suspicious of Robin's friends, believing them to be a bad influence on him. Now he felt that his father accepted them more and that in some subtle way, they were viewed as part of his social circle rather than 'a gang' that might lead him astray. But his own perspective had changed. In some ways he felt more detached from home and his parents' views and found himself able to contemplate for the first time the possibility of a move away from home which wouldn't inevitably lead to the end of his relationship with his parents. At times it was difficult to believe just how angry with them he had been, though he could remember the terrible rows which led him to feel that he had no option but to leave for good. Now, three years later he felt more in control. He felt that after a great deal of hard work by himself and his parents, he was able to have his own life and still keep contact with home life. As a bonus, relationships between himself and his father in particular had improved immeasurably. There were conflicts of course, particularly over his studies. He was reconciled to the fact that he was no academic and would always prefer social activities. Nevertheless, he felt that he had been able to keep up with other students and he was reasonably confident about the outcome of his recent public examinations. He hoped that next year would give him the opportunity to do voluntary work, mainly away from home. He remained unsure as to whether or not he would go to university. He was aware that his parents would be disappointed if he did not go, but he felt that it was a decision he wanted to give further thought to rather than enter into lightly. Overall, he felt he had matured. His uncle who had remained in touch throughout this difficult period, agreed.

The reflections of Robin are not everyone's story of adolescence, of course, as some of the illustrations in this book have demonstrated. As we have seen throughout this book, many teenagers go through a wild and tormenting time, causing great turmoil for themselves and often the whole family. The search for a new identity often leads to rebellion as they turn against received values and against any kind of pressure which, it is felt, may restrict this new freedom. At this time it is crucial to feel the strong support of parents and adults who may not approve of everything they do but who nevertheless stick by them when it matters, and thus help to provide the containing space within which strong foundations for adult life can be laid down and developed.

FURTHER READING

Box, S. (ed) et al, *Crisis at Adolescence: Object Relations Therapy with the Family*. Jason Aronson Inc., New Jersey & London, 1994.

Copley, B., *The world of adolescence. Literature, society and psychoanalytic psychotherapy*. London Free Association Books, 1993.

Copley, B. and Forryan, B., *Therapeutic work with children and young people*. London, Robert Royce, 1987.

Salzberger-Wittenberg, I., *Psychoanalytic insight and relationships. A Kleinian approach*. London, Routledge & Kegan Paul, 1970.

Salzberger-Wittenberg, I., et al, *The emotional experience of learning and teaching*. London, Routledge & Kegan Paul, 1983.

HELPFUL ORGANISATIONS

Angel Drugs Project, 33–44 Liverpool Road, Islington, London N1 0171 226 3113

Childline, 2nd Floor, Royal Mail Building, Studd Street, London N1 0QW 0800 1111 (Freephone for children) or 0171 239 1000

Exploring Parenthood, Freepost, 194 Freston Road, London W10 6BR. 0181 960 1678 (Parents' Advice Line)

Young Minds, 22a Boston Place, London NW1 6ER 0171 724 7262 (National Advisory Clinic)

Release (Criminal Legal Drug Service), 388 Old St, London EC1V 9LT 0171 729 9904

Turning Point, 101 Backchurch Lane, London E1 1LU 0171 702 2300

Brook Advisory Services, Birth Control Clinics, 0171 617 8000 (24 hour automated helpline)

The Anti Bullying Campaign, 10 Borough High St, London SE1 9QQ 0171 378 1446

The Eating Disorders Association, Sackville Place, 44–8 Magdalen St, Norwich, Norfolk NR3 1JE 0603 765050

Gingerbread, 35 Wellington St, London WC2E 7BN 0171 240 0953

The National Stepfamily Association, 72 Willesden Lane, London NW6 7TA 0171 372 0848

Lifeline for Parents, 103–3 Oldham St, Manchester M41 LW 0800 716701 (Freephone helpline Mon–Thurs 5pm–9pm)

Adfam, 0171 638 3700 (Mon–Fri 10am–5pm)

Families Anonymous, The Doddington & Rolo's Community Association, Charlotte Despard Ave, London SW11 5JE 0171 498 4680

In London

Young People's Counselling Service (over 16's), a self-referral service for adolescents.

Tavistock Clinic, 120 Belsize Lane, NW3 5BA (Tel: 0171 435 7111 ext 2337)

UNDERSTANDING YOUR CHILD

ORDER FORM FOR TITLES IN THIS SERIES

Send to: Rosendale Press Ltd., Premier House
10 Greycoat Place, London SW1P 1SB

Price per volume: £5.75 inc. post & packing

Understanding Your Baby by Lisa Miller	. . . . . copies
Understanding Your 1 Year Old by Deborah Steiner	. . . . . copies
Understanding Your 2 Year Old by Susan Reid	. . . . . copies
Understanding Your 3 Year Old by Judith Trowell	. . . . . copies
Understanding Your 4 Year Old by Lisa Miller	. . . . . copies
Understanding Your 5 Year Old by Lesley Holditch	. . . . . copies
Understanding Your 6 Year Old by Deborah Steiner	. . . . . copies
Understanding Your 7 Year Old by Elsie Osborne	. . . . . copies
Understanding Your 8 Year Old by Lisa Miller	. . . . . copies
Understanding Your 9 Year Old by Dora Lush	. . . . . copies
Understanding Your 10 Year Old by Jonathan Bradley	. . . . . copies
Understanding Your 11 Year Old by Eileen Orford	. . . . . copies
Understanding Your Handicapped Child by Valerie Sinason	. . . . . copies
Understanding 12–14 Year Olds by Margot Waddell	. . . . . copies
Understanding 15–17 Years Old by Hélène Dubinsky & Jonathan Bradley	. . . . . copies
Understanding 18–20 Year Olds by Gianna Williams & Beta Copley	. . . . . copies

Total amount enclosed: £. . . . .
Name . . . .
Address . . . .
. . . . Post code . . . .